# Breakthrough English

# PREFACE

이 책은 기초부터 시작하고 싶거나 해외여행 시에 혹은 취업이나 시험을 준비하는 대학생들에게 도움이 될 수 있는 책을 만들고자 하는 의도에서 펴내게 된 것입니다.

우선 실생활에서 부딪치는 상황별 회화를 통해 외국어 의사소통 능력을 향상시키는데 가장 큰 목표를 두었습니다.

또한 단어와 문법을 정리하고 실전문제를 풀 수 있도록 구성함으로써 전반적인 영어능력 향상을 가져올 수 있도록 엮었습니다.

그리고 자기소개서, 편지와 이메일, 인터뷰 등에 대처할 수 있도록 특별히 선별한 내용을 수록하였습니다.

마지막으로 외국어 의사소통능력 향상을 위해 다양한 연습문제를 통한 효율적인 학습을 목표로 만들어진 본 교재가 영어실력 향상을 가져올 수 있는 계기와 그 기초를 마련하는 초석이 되기를 바랍니다.

2017년 8월

저자 씀

# CONTENTS

# Unit 1 Telephone

# Vocabulary

- repair shop　　수리점
- secretary　　비서
- available　　이용 가능한
- hold　　수화기를 들고 기다리다
- direct　　방향을 정하다
- vacation　　휴가
- receptionist　　접수계원
- client　　고객
- appointment　　약속
- instead　　대신에

## Dialogue 1

Mechanic / Client

Mechanic: Hyundai Auto Repair Shop. How may I help you?

Client: Good morning. May I speak to Mr. Kim?

Mechanic: He is not in here. May I ask who is calling?

Client: This is Lee Hun. May I leave a message?

Mechanic: Sure. Go ahead.

Client: Would you ask him to call me when he comes back?

Mechanic: Yes. Does he know your number?

Client: Yes, he knows.

## Dialogue 2

Secretary Businessman

Secretary: Good morning. Ms. Kim's office.

Businessman: May I speak to her, please?

Secretary: I'll check if she's available.

Businessman: Okay, I'll hold.

Secretary: I'm sorry, she's on another line right now. May I ask who's calling?

Businessman: This is Mr. Lee.

Secretary: Would you like to hold for a moment or try again later?

Businessman: I'll call later, thank you.

## Dialogue 3

Secretary　Businessman

Secretary: Good morning, Mr. Brown's office. How may I direct your call?

Businessman: Hello, this is Tom Smith. May I speak with Mr. Brown?

Secretary: I'm sorry, he's on leave now.

Businessman: Where has he gone to?

Secretary: He went to Nepal for a vacation.

Businessman: When do you expect him back?

Secretary: He should be back in about two weeks. Can I take a message?

Businessman: No, that's all right. I'll call again later.

## Dialogue 4

Receptionist  Client

Hello. How may I help you?

Hello. I'd like to make an appointment for a perm.
Could you connect me to Mike, my hair designer?

Let me check. Sorry, he is off today.

Is there the head of department instead?

Yes, would you like to schedule an appointment?

How about 3 o'clock in the afternoon?

Okay. I'll put you down for 3 PM today. May I have your name, please?

My name is Kim, Hanseul.

Your reservation is done. We'll be waiting for you. Good-bye!

## Comprehension Check-Up

**Write the answer to the question in English.**

Q1. May I speak to Mr. Kim?

A1. ________________________________________.

Q2. Would you ask him to call me when he comes back?

A2. ________________________________________.

Q3. Would you like to hold for a moment or try again later?

A3. ________________________________________.

Q4. Mr. Brown's office. How may I direct your call?

A4. ________________________________________.

Q5. Where has he gone to?

A5. ________________________________________.

Q6. Could you connect me to Mike, my hair designer?

A6. ________________________________________.

Q7. Would you like to schedule an appointment?

A7. ________________________________________.

## Translate into English

1. 전화하시는 분은 누구신지요?

2. 그가 당신의 전화번호를 아시나요?

3. 그분은 다른 전화를 받고 있습니다.

4. 잠시 전화를 끊지 말고 기다리시겠어요?

5. 나중에 다시 걸겠습니다.

6. 죄송하지만, 그분은 오늘 비번입니다.

7. 오늘 오후 3시에 예약로 적어 놓겠습니다.

## Vocabulary Hunting

**Fill in the space for the word that fits best in the sentence.**

(hold, available, appointment, about, expect, vacation, leave)

1. I'll check if she's (                    ).

2. He went to Nepal for a (                    ).

3. When do you (                    ) him back?

4. I'd like to make an (                    ) for a perm.

5. Would you like to (                    ) for a moment or try again later?

6. May I (                    ) a message?

7. How (                    ) 3 o'clock in the afternoon?

# Grammar Test 1

## 1. 동사 (Verb)

**Key Points**

1. 문장에서 주어와 동사가 무엇인지를 파악한다.
2. 5가지 문장 유형과 각 유형별 동사들의 특징을 이해한다.
3. 사역동사와 지각동사의 목적격 보어로 쓰일 때는 원형부정사(동사원형)를 쓴다.
4. 다음의 관용어구 다음에는 원형부정사를 쓴다.
   had better(~하는 편이 낫다), cannot but(~하지 않을 수 없다),
   would rather(차라리 ~하겠다), may well(~하는 것이 당연하다),
   do nothing but(~하기만 하다)
5. '목적어 + to 부정사(5형식)'에서 목적어가 부정사의 의미상의 주어가 된다.
   I expect him to work hard.

## Choose the best form to fill the gap

**1. Because there were no chairs, all of us ________ on the floor.**

① sat ② seat
③ set ④ was seated

**2. I never feel very ________ when I walk along that street.**

① safely ② safety
③ safe ④ save

**3. Please ________ your hand if you have any questions.**

① press ② arise
③ raise ④ rose

**4. She explained ________.**

① me the matter ② to me the matter
③ the matter of me ④ the matter for me

**5. I had my composition ________ by our professor.**

① correcting ② correct
③ corrective ④ corrected

# Vocabulary Test 1

**1. You can find information about both past and ________ events in the newsletter.**

① upcoming ② invitation
③ farewell ④ informal

**2. I will ________ the mike to our host for the event.**

① send ② hand over
③ turn on ④ hand in

**3. An ________ employee is a role model for the other coworkers.**

① prestigious ② famous
③ exemplary(모범적인) ④ standing

**4. We ask that you kindly ________ all mobile phones in the cabin.**

① turn on ② attend on
③ put on ④ turn off

**5. We could ________ the food to your house at 7pm.**

① deliver ② content
③ help ④ pack

Breakthrough English

# Unit 2 Directions

# Vocabulary

- directions 길안내
- detail 세부적 내용
- shuttle bus 근거리 왕복버스
- straight 똑바로
- traffic light 신호등
- appreciate 고마워하다
- lost 길 잃은, 난감해진
- repeat 반복하다
- catch 이해하다, 잡다
- department store 백화점

## Dialogue 1

Information Desk    Student

Information Desk: Information Desk. How may I help you?

Student: Good morning. Would you tell me how to get to Kookje College?

Information Desk: Where are you coming from?

Student: I am coming from Seoul.

Information Desk: You had better take a subway Line One to Seojungri Station.

Student: Would you give me directions in detail?

Information Desk: Leave by Songtan City Hall Exit at Seojungri Staton. And you can use Kookje College shuttle bus or the bus no.55 in front of the station.

Student: How long does it take from the station?

Information Desk: It takes about 10 minutes by bus.

Student: Thank you for your kindness.

Information Desk: My pleasure.

## Dialogue 2

Passenger one　Passenger two

Passenger one: Excuse me. Could you give me some directions?

Passenger two: Certainly. What are you looking for?

Passenger one: I need to buy a stapler at a stationery store.

Passenger two: Well, there's one about three blocks away on Rodeo Street.

Passenger one: How do I get there?

Passenger two: Walk straight until you come to the first traffic light. Then turn left, and Kyobo bookstore will be on the right side. You can find a stationery store in the bookstore.

Passenger one: I appreciate your help.

Passenger two: You're welcome.

## Dialogue 3

Passenger one　Passenger two

(Passenger one) Which street am I on now?

(Passenger two) You're on Rodeo street. You look a little lost. Can I help you?

(Passenger one) Thanks. I'm trying to find City Hall. Is it right to take a subway here for City Hall?

(Passenger two) It's not far from here. Just walk up this street about two blocks and take a left. City Hall will be on your right side.

(Passenger one) I didn't catch that. Could you repeat that again?

(Passenger two) Just walk up two blocks and take a left.

(Passenger one) Did you say two blocks?

(Passenger two) Right. Two blocks and turn left. You can't miss it.

(Passenger one) I think I can find it. Thanks for your help.

## Dialogue 4

Passenger 1 Passenger 2

Passenger 1: Excuse me. How do I get to the nearest Department Store?

Passenger 2: There is one after five blocks from here.

Passenger 1: Is this the right bus stop for the department store?

Passenger 2: No, it isn't. You should go to the opposite direction.

Passenger 1: Great. And where can I find the restroom?

Passenger 2: You can find it in the subway station right over there.

Passenger 1: Just one last question. Would you happen to know if there is a movie theater nearby?

Passenger 2: Sure, there is one on the third floor in the SM Mall.

Passenger 1: I appreciate your help. Have a good day!

## Comprehension Check-Up

**Write the answer to the question in English.**

Q1. Would you tell me how to get to Kookje College?

A1. ______________________________.

Q2. How long does it take from the station?

A2. ______________________________.

Q3. What are you looking for?

A3. ______________________________.

Q4. Which street am I on now?

A4. ______________________________.

Q5. How do I get to the nearest Department Store?

A5. ______________________________.

Q6. Is this the right bus stop for the department store?

A6. ______________________________.

Q7. Would you happen to know if there is a movie theater nearby?

A7. ______________________________.

## Translate into English

1. 국제대학에 가는 방법을 말씀해주시겠어요?

2. 기차역으로부터 얼마나 걸리나요?

3. 실례지만, 길안내를 해주시겠어요?

4. 도와주셔서 고마워요.

5. 지금 내가 어떤 도로 위에 있는 건가요?

6. 당신은 그것을 놓칠 리가 없어요.

7. 화장실이 어디에 있나요?

## Vocabulary Hunting

**Fill in the space for the word that fits best in the sentence.**

(repeat, three, third, get, straight, take, give)

1. I didn't catch that. Could you (            ) that again?

2. Well, there's one about (            ) blocks away on Rodeo Street.

3. How long does it (            ) from the station?

4. Excuse me. Could you (            ) me some directions?

5. Walk (            ) until you come to the first traffic light.

6. Sure, there is one on the (            ) floor in the SM Mall.

7. How do I (            ) to the nearest Department Store?

# Grammar Test 2

## 2. 시제 (Tense)

**● Key Points**

1. 시제는 동작이나 상태가 나타날 때의 시간적 위치이다.
2. 시간이나 조건을 나타내는 부사절에서는 미래시제 대신 현재시제를 쓴다.
3. 주절의 동사와 종속절의 동사는 시제를 일치시킨다.

## Choose the best form to fill the gap

**1. I am afraid that it ________ tomorrow.**

① rains ② rained
③ is raining ④ will rain

**2. Turn off the lights when you ________ the room.**

① leave ② leaving
③ left ④ have left

**3. The plane ________ at 5:00 p.m. tomorrow.**

① plane ② has left
③ is leaving ④ has gone

**4. The museum ________ ten years ago.**

① built ② has been built
③ has built ④ was built

**5. By the time he gets home, his wife ________ for Canada.**

① will leave ② will have left
③ leaves ④ is leaving

## Vocabulary Test 2

**1. I eat an apple every day. It is my ________ treat.**

① daily ② vegetable
③ black ④ delicious

**2. The sky is full of color as the sun goes down. It is ________.**

① sunrise ② sunset
③ noon ④ morning

**3. Are you looking for a ________ cheese or an imported one?**

① final ② delivered
③ bargain ④ domestic(국내의)

**4. We have received your registration form and ________.**

① information ② pack
③ patronage(후원, 애용) ④ deposit(보증금)

**5. This product is ________ at retail(소매상의) stores only.**

① good ② flexible
③ accept ④ available

Breakthrough English

# Unit 3 Shopping

# Vocabulary

| | |
|---|---|
| pants | 바지 |
| waist | 허리 |
| length | 기장 |
| heater | 난방기 |
| browse | 살펴보다 |
| quite | 매우 |
| rage | 대유행 |
| fitting room | 탈의실 |
| certainly | 물론이지 |
| visit | 방문하다 |

## Dialogue 1

Clerk Customer

Clerk: Hello. May I help you?

Customer: I'm looking for some pants.

Clerk: What size do you take?

Customer: A 33 waist and a 36 length.

Clerk: How do you like this pair?

Customer: Can you show me others?

Clerk: How about this one?

Customer: They look fine. Can I try them on?

Clerk: Absolutely. The dressing room is right over there.

# Dialogue 2

Clerk / Customer

**Clerk:** Good morning. Can I help you?

**Customer:** Yes. I bought this heater here yesterday, but it doesn't work.

**Clerk:** What's wrong with it?

**Customer:** I don't know. I took it home, plugged it in, turned it on, and nothing happened.

**Clerk:** Do you have a receipt?

**Customer:** Yes, here it is.

**Clerk:** OK, I'll get you another one.

**Customer:** I'd like a refund.

**Clerk:** All right, I'll see what I can do.

## Dialogue 3

Clerk Customer

Clerk: What are you looking for, ma'am?

Customer: I'm just browsing for some fur coats.

Clerk: Solid pink is quite the rage. Why don't you try it on?

Customer: But it looks too loud. Do you have anything brown?

Clerk: How about this one? This dark brown is brand new.

Customer: I'll try it on. Where is the fitting room?

Clerk: Right this way, please.

Customer: Do you think this goes well with me?

Clerk: It looks good on you.

Customer: OK. I'll take it. How much is it?

Clerk: It comes to nine hundred dollars including tax.

## Dialogue 4

Clerk Customer

Clerk: Hello. Is there anything I can help you?

Customer: Yes. Can you show me some with TV sets?

Clerk: Certainly, sir. What make would you like?

Customer: I'd like a LG.

Clerk: This one is very excellent. It is a new model.

Customer: I'm looking for a smaller sized one.

Clerk: This is the smallest one we have.

Customer: Then I'll look around more.

Clerk: Thank you for visiting anyway. Please come again.

## Comprehension Check-Up

**Write the answer to the question in English.**

Q1. Can I try them on?

A1. ______________________________________________.

Q2. Do you have a receipt?

A2. ______________________________________________.

Q3. What are you looking for, ma'am?

A3. ______________________________________________.

Q4. I'll try it on. Where is the fitting room?

A4. ______________________________________________.

Q5. Do you think this goes well with me?

A5. ______________________________________________.

Q6. I'll take it. How much is it?

A6. ______________________________________________.

Q7. What brand would you like?

A7. ______________________________________________.

## Translate into English

1. 나는 바지를 구입하려고 합니다.

_______________________________________________

2. 무슨 사이즈를 원하나요?

_______________________________________________

3. 그것을 입어 봐도 되나요?

_______________________________________________

4. 이 난방기가 작동을 안 합니다.

_______________________________________________

5. 영수증을 가지고 있나요?

_______________________________________________

6. 나는 환불을 원합니다.

_______________________________________________

7. 이것이 나에게 어울린다고 생각하나요?.

_______________________________________________

## Vocabulary Hunting

**Fill in the space for the word that fits best in the sentence.**

(is, with, like, work, another, on, sized)

1. Do you think this goes well (          ) me?

2. The dressing room (          ) right over there.

3. I bought this heater here yesterday, but it doesn't (          ).

4. Can I try them (          )?

5. I'm looking for a smaller (          ) one.

6. I'll get you (          ) one.

7. How do you (          ) this pair?

# Grammar Test 3

## 3. 태 (Voice)

**● Key Points**

1. 주어가 동작을 행하면 능동태, 주어가 동작을 받으면 수동태를 쓴다.
2. 모든 자동사 및 resemble, have, cost 등의 동사들은 수동태를 만들 수 없다.
3. 수동태는 "by + 목적격"을 쓰지만 by 이외의 전치사를 쓰는 동사들도 있다.

## Choose the best form to fill the gap

**1. Taking photographs ______________ in this building.**

① can not allow ② has not permission

③ is not allowed ④ doesn't allow

**2. The city is run _________ the mayor.**

① to ② by

③ from ④ with

**3. I was surprised _________ the news.**

① for ② to

③ at ④ from

**4. Mt. Everest is known _________ all of us for its natural beauty.**

① to ② for

③ in ④ with

**5. The students _________ at exactly nine o'clock.**

① arriving ② were arrival

③ were arrived ④ arrived

# Vocabulary Test 3

**1. Please ________ a copy of the receipt for your records.**

① distribute ② contract
③ trade ④ retain

**2. Samsung is enjoying ________ growth in all international markets.**

① stable ② well
③ unemployed ④ unavoidable

**3. The new free trade agreement will ________ exports.**

① start ② excite
③ increased ④ boost

**4. We offer the most ________ prices on office supplies.**

① valid ② attractive
③ resonable ④ competition

**5. Once you _______a credit card , It is important that you use it wisely.**

① obtain ② produce
③ attract ④ replace

Breakthrough English

# Unit 4 Fashion

## Vocabulary

| | |
|---|---|
| fashion outlet | 의류 직매점 |
| bus fare | 버스요금 |
| run | 운행하다 |
| average | 평균 |
| see-through | 비쳐 보이는 스타일 |
| chiffon | 비단이나 레이온처럼 결이 고운 |
| alter | 변경하다 |
| formal | 정장 |
| heel | 뒤꿈치 |
| popular | 인기 있는 |

## Dialogue 1

Customer · Information Desk

**Customer:** Could you tell me where I can take the subway to your Fashion Outlet from Leechun City Hall?

**Information Desk:** You should get off at the second bus stop. And walk to the subway nearby for five minutes. You can transfer to the subway there.

**Customer:** What line should I take?

**Information Desk:** Line two, the green line. You need to get off at the third stop and take a shuttle bus in front of the Leesom Hotel.

**Customer:** Do you know how often the buses run?

**Information Desk:** About an average of 10 minutes.

**Customer:** By the way, what's the bus fare?

**Information Desk:** It will be one thousand won.

**Customer:** Thank you very much. Have a nice day.

## Dialogue 2

Clerk Customer

Clerk: How may I help you?

Customer: I'm looking for some see-through look.

Clerk: That should be at no.4 section right over there.

Customer: Oh, I see. I'll take a look.

Clerk: Excuse me, can I get this in smaller size, please?

Customer: Sure, which one would you like?

Clerk: I would like this chiffon blouse with a red tone.

Customer: Okay, I'll check if we have a size for you.

## Dialogue 3

Clerk / Customer

Clerk: How can I help you?

Customer: Yes, please. I like this dress, but do you have a smaller size?

Clerk: Sorry, that's the last one.

Customer: Well, can I have it altered then?

Clerk: Of course. What would you like to do?

Customer: Could you take in the waist?

Clerk: All right.

Customer: How long will it take?

Clerk: It will be prepared by the day after tomorrow.

Customer: Fine, thank you.

## Dialogue 4

Clerk Customer

Clerk: Hi, may I help you find something?

Customer: I'm looking for some shoes.

Clerk: What kind of shoes do you want?

Customer: I want something formal.

Clerk: How about these nice high heels?

Customer: I don't like that color.
Maybe I'll just go somewhere else.

Clerk: Wait, please. We have other shoes.

Customer: Like what?

Clerk: Here. This is one of our popular styles.

Customer: Great.

## Comprehension Check-Up

**Write the answer to the question in English.**

Q1. Do you know how often the buses run?

A1. ________________________________________.

Q2. What's the bus fare?

A2. ________________________________________.

Q3. Which one would you like?

A3. ________________________________________.

Q4. I like this dress, but do you have a smaller size?

A4. ________________________________________.

Q5. Well, can I have it altered then?

A5. ________________________________________.

Q6. Hi, may I help you find something?

A6. ________________________________________.

Q7. What kind of shoes do you want?

A7. ________________________________________.

## Translate into English

1. 도보로 5분 걸릴 겁니다.

2. 얼마나 자주 버스가 운행하는지 아시나요?

3. 나는 시스루룩을 구하려고 합니다.

4. 허리를 줄여주시겠어요?

5. 그것은 모레쯤 준비될 것입니다.

6. 당신은 어떤 종류의 구두를 원하나요?

7. 이 하이힐은 어떤가요?

## Vocabulary Hunting

**Fill in the space for the word that fits best in the sentence.**

(look, popular, run, waist, formal, fare, kind)

1. What (                ) of shoes do you want?

2. Could you take in the (                )?

3. By the way, what's the bus (                )?

4. Do you know how often the buses (                )?

5. I'm looking for some see-through (                ).

6. This is one of our (                ) styles.

7. I want something (                )

# Grammar Test 4

## 4. 법(Subjunctive Mood)

**● Key Points**

1. 법에는 직설법, 명령법, 가정법이 있는데, 가정법은 어떤 사실을 상상, 소망, 또는 의문하여 가정하는 것이다.
2. 가정법 현재(불확실한 사실을 가정 '~라면 ~할 것이다') 과거(현실과 반대되는 상황 '~라면 ~할 텐데'), 과거 완료(과거 사실과 반대되는 가정 '~했더라면 ~했을 텐데', 미래(강한 의심)의 형식과 용법을 암기한다.
3. 가정법 문장에서 if가 생략되면, 주어와 동사의 어순이 바뀐다.

## Choose the best form to fill the gap

**1. The party will be canceled ________ it rains tomorrow morning.**

① unless ② if
③ had ④ otherwise

**2. If you ________ to see Miss Kim, what would you tell her?**

① are ② will be going
③ must ④ were

**3. If they provided some information, we ________ more money.**

① would have earned ② earn
③ would earn ④ earned

**4. "Your performance was very good."**
**"I could have done better ________ more time."**

① I had ② had I
③ had I had ④ I have had

**5. ________ a lot of money, he could not have bought the house.**

① Without ② Nevertheless
③ If ④ But

# Vocabulary Test 4

**1. With this coupon, you can receive 20% discount off of your next ________ .**

① purchase ② month
③ reduce ④ price

**2. I like to use fresh ________ from the farm when I cook.**

① thing ② produce(농작물)
③ food ④ fish

**3. Please visit any of ________ locations throughout the downtown area.**

① convenient ② peak
③ short ④ ready

**4. We will ________ any defective product free of charge.**

① replace ② consider
③ valuable ④ put

**5. The head chef has more than 30 years of ________ experience.**

① recipe ② ingredient
③ culinary ④ dinner

# Unit 5 Skin Care

# Vocabulary

- facial treatment 안면 관리
- pricy 값비싼(pricey)
- exfoliation 박리
- facial product 화장품
- pimple 뾰루지, 여드름(zit)
- pop 터트리다
- scar 흉터
- eczema 습진
- chronic 만성의
- dermatologist 피부과 전문의

## Dialogue 1

Friend 1 Friend 2

(Friend 1) Where are you going?

(Friend 2) I'm going to get a facial at 11 o'clock.

(Friend 1) Do you get facials often?

(Friend 2) Not really. Once a month.

(Friend 1) Does your skin get better when you get one?

(Friend 2) Of course. I can feel the difference right away.

(Friend 1) Why don't you get them more often?

(Friend 2) Well, facials are a bit pricy.

(Friend 1) What kind of facial do you get?

(Friend 2) I normally get a full facial treatment. It includes a face massage, exfoliation, and a basic moisturizing mask.

# Dialogue 2

Friend 1 Friend 2

Friend 1: My face is flaky.

Friend 2: Your skin gets very dry in the winter. You have to use lotion.

Friend 1: I put on lotion every day.

Friend 2: What kind of lotion do you use?

Friend 1: I'm not sure which brand it is. Someone gave it to me as a gift.

Friend 2: What kind of facial products do you use?

Friend 1: I just put on aftershave and lotion.

Friend 2: Don't you use sunscreen, serum, toner, or BB Cream?

Friend 1: No, I don't like my face being oily.

Friend 2: Using sun-block is quite important because UV rays are very bad for your skin. You have to apply sunscreen every 5 hours.

## Dialogue 3

Friend 1 Friend 2

My face is breaking out these days.

Are those pimples?

I don't know what they are.

Are you getting a lot of stress these days?

No, but I'm not getting enough sleep.

Then that's probably why.
I heard good sleep is really important for your skin.

Plus, I have oily skin. I get zits like this every now and then.

You shouldn't pop zits yourself for they may leave scars. You'd better go to the doctor if it gets worse.

Yeah, I think I will.

## Dialogue 4

Friend 1 Friend 2

Friend 1: What's wrong with your skin?

Friend 2: I have a skin condition called atopy.

Friend 1: Is it serious?

Friend 2: Well, it gets worse sometimes.

Friend 1: That looks painful.

Friend 2: It's not painful, but it is a little itchy.

Friend 1: I also used to get eczema quite often.

Friend 2: I used to get that when I was a kid, too.

Friend 1: What do you do to treat your atopy?

Friend 2: Well, it's a chronic condition. I go to the dermatologist to get medication when it gets bad.

## Comprehension Check-Up

**Write the answer to the question in English.**

Q1. Where are you going?

A1. ______________________________.

Q2. Do you get facials often?

A2. ______________________________.

Q3. Does your skin get better when you get a facial?

A3. ______________________________.

Q4. What kind of facial products do you use?

A4. ______________________________.

Q5. Are you getting a lot of stress these days?

A5. ______________________________.

Q6. What's wrong with your skin?

A6. ______________________________.

Q7. What do you do to treat your atopy?

A7. ______________________________.

## Translate into English

1. 당신은 어디에 가십니까?

2. 나는 11시에 안면관리를 받을 겁니다.

3. 나는 매일 로션을 바릅니다.

4. 당신은 5시간마다 선크림을 발라야합니다.

5. 당신은 여드름을 직접 짜면 안 됩니다.

6. 나는 아토피 피부를 가지고 있어요.

7. 나는 때때로 약물치료를 받기위해 피부과 전문의에게 갑니다.

## Vocabulary Hunting

**Fill in the space for the word that fits best in the sentence.**

(pop, treat, facial, put, apply, bit, painful)

1. You shouldn't ( ) zits yourself.

2. I'm going to get a ( ) at 11 o'clock.

3. What do you do to ( ) your atopy?

4. You have to ( ) sunscreen every 5 hours.

5. It's not ( ), but it is a little itchy.

6. I ( ) on lotion every day.

7. Well, facials are a ( ) pricy.

# Grammar Test 5

## 5. 부정사 (Infinitive)

### Key Points

1. 준동사(to 부정사, 동명사, 분사) 중 하나이며 형태상 부정사(to+동사원형)와 원형부정사(to를 쓰지 않고 동사원형만 씀)가 있다.
2. to 부정사를 목적어로 취하는 동사 : want, wish, hope, expect, intend, agree, promise, plan, decide, refuse 등의 동사 들이 있다.
   to 부정사를 목적격 보어로 취하는 동사 : expect, persuade, ask, enable, cause, order, allow, force, encourage, believe 등의 동사 들이 있다.
3. 지각동사, 사역동사의 목적격 보어로 쓰일 때는 원형부정사를 쓴다. (help는 둘 다 가능)

## Choose the best form to fill the gap

**1. "그 아이에게 가지고 놀 장난감을 주어라."의 옳은 영역은?**

① Give the child a toy to play with.

② Give the child a toy to play.

③ Give the child a toy playing.

④ Give the child a toy to be playing.

**2. He has no one ________ but himself.**

① to blame to　　② of blame

③ to blame　　④ blaming for

**3. They found the plan difficult ________.**

① to be carried out　　② to carry out

③ being carried out　　④ carrying out

**4. We expect ________ a department store with a larger parking lot.**

① building　　② build

③ to build　　④ to building

**5. Money enables us ________ a lot of things.**

① to have done　　② do

③ doing　　④ to do

## Vocabulary Test 5

**1. They use only the freshest ________ in all their dishes.**

① flavors ② fat
③ frozen ④ ingredients

**2. Some of the coworkers have ________ a carpool to reduce their fuel costs.**

① seat ② ride
③ arranged ④ separated

**3. The airline is well known for its _________.**

① booking ② history
③ access ④ hospitality

**4. Come and enjoy a ________ at the library this weekend.**

① compose ② remind
③ film ④ study

**5. A visit to an art gallery will ________ our life.**

① sad ② enrich
③ run ④ good

# Unit 6 Medical

# Vocabulary

- nurse 간호사
- patient 환자
- annual 해마다, 연례의
- physical examination 건강검진(checkup)
- opening 빈 시간
- schedule 일정을 계획하다
- chart 기록표
- cavity 충치
- molar tooth 어금니
- crown 크라운유리
- numb 무감각해진(benumbed)
- relief 안도, 안심

# Dialogue 1

Nurse Patient

Nurse: Hello. How may I help you?

Patient: I would like to make an appointment with Dr. Kim, please.

Nurse: What would you like to see him for?

Patient: I need my annual physical examination.

Nurse: Dr. Kim has opening next week. Are you free on Monday or Tuesday?

Patient: I'm free on Monday morning.

Nurse: We will schedule you for next Monday.

## Dialogue 2

Nurse Patient

Nurse: Is this your first time to our office?

Patient: Yes, it is my first time here.

Nurse: Could you fill out this chart, please?

Patient: Sure.

Nurse: How can we help you today?

Patient: I have a cavity on my molar tooth.

Nurse: Let me see it. I see that the molar broke off.

Patient: Do I need a crown?

Nurse: I think it is best to treat it with a crown.

Patient: Is it going to hurt?

Nurse: You won't feel a thing. I am going to make the tooth numb first.

Patient: That's a relief.

## Dialogue 3

Doctor Patient

(Doctor) How are you? What made you come in today?

(Patient) My stomach hurts.

(Doctor) How long have you had this symptom?

(Patient) It has lasted for a couple of days.

(Doctor) Let me examine you. Do you feel any pain when I palpitate your stomach?

(Patient) Yes, I feel a little pain.

(Doctor) Have you ever thrown up?

(Patient) I have vomited yesterday night.

(Doctor) You may have a mild stomach ulcer. I'll write a prescription for some medicine.

(Patient) Thanks, Doctor.

## Dialogue 4

Patient's mom　Doctor

Patient's mom: Dr. Jung, what's wrong with my son?

Doctor: He's got the flu. I want you to monitor his temperature.

Patient's mom: How often should I check it?

Doctor: Once every 3 hours.

Patient's mom: What about the diet?

Doctor: Regular food is okay, but avoid heavy foods.

Patient's mom: Is there anything else that I need to take care of?

Doctor: Yeah. Make sure you visit me so that I can have a look at him again after two days.

Patient's mom: You bet. Thanks.

## Comprehension Check-Up

**Write the answer to the question in English.**

Q1. What would you like to see him for?

A1. ______________________________.

Q2. Is this your first time to our office?

A2. ______________________________.

Q3. Do I need a crown?

A3. ______________________________.

Q4. What made you come in today?

A4. ______________________________.

Q5. Have you ever thrown up?

A5. ______________________________.

Q6. Dr. Jung, what's wrong with my son?

A6. ______________________________.

Q7. Is there anything else that I need to take care of?

A7. ______________________________.

## Translate into English

1. 김 박사님과 진료예약을 하려고 합니다.

2. 김 박사님은 오늘 예약이 꽉 차있습니다.

3. 다음 주 월요일에 일정을 잡도록 하겠습니다.

4. 이 진료기록표를 작성해 주시겠어요?

5. 이 증상이 얼마나 오래 되었나요?

6. 토하신 적이 있나요?

7. 보통 음식을 드세요, 그러나 기름진 음식은 피하세요.

## Vocabulary Hunting

**Fill in the space for the word that fits best in the sentence.**

(cavity, avoid, symptom, like, prescription, lasted, stomach)

1. Regular food is okay, but (                ) heavy foods.

2. What would you (                ) to see him for?

3. I have a (                ) on my molar tooth.

4. How long have you had this (                )?

5. It has (                ) for a couple of days.

6. You may have a mild (                ) ulcer.

7. I'll write a (                ) for some medicine.

# Grammar Test 6

## 6. 동명사 (Gerund)

**Key Points**

1. 동명사는 동사의 변이형으로 명사의 속성을 지닌다.
2. 동사가 전치사의 목적어로 쓰이면 반드시 동명사를 써야 한다.
3. 동명사만을 목적어로 취하는 동사들을 암기한다.
   enjoy, finish, mind, give up, consider, avoid, postpone, deny, stop

## Choose the best form to fill the gap

**1. I enjoyed ________ a book in the library.**

① to reading ② to read
③ read ④ reading

**2. I can't imagine ________ in an examination.**

① he failing ② his failing
③ him failing ④ he fail to

**3. We had a hard time ________ his office.**

① to finding ② find
③ finding ④ at finding

**4. Randy is sick. ___________ all night in the rain caused him to catch a cold.**

① His working ② Him to work
③ He working ④ He worked

**5. He is looking forward ________ his brothers in Chicago.**

① to meet ② for meeting
③ to meeting ④ in meeting

# Vocabulary Test 6

**1. Many people think that gold is an excellent ________.**

① investment ② interest

③ facility ④ account

**2. The company ________ s a total of 7 million dollars to the bank.**

① give ② owe

③ saved ④ cash

**3. This safety ________ will prevent you from falling off the roof.**

① cap ② railing(난간)

③ wings ④ building

**4. People are impressed by the ________ appearance of the building.**

① furnished ② value

③ distinctive ④ practical

**5. Please take all deliveries to the rear ________ of the building.**

① rent ② structure

③ neighborhood ④ entrance

# Unit 7 Surgery

## Vocabulary

- sagging 처짐
- prevent 막다
- outpatient 외래의
- complicated 복잡한
- surgery 수술
- anesthesia 마취
- syndrome 증후군
- blink 깜박이다
- satisfy 만족시키다
- requisite 필요조건
- recently 최근에
- crease 주름

## Dialogue 1

Doctor Robin　Patient

(Doctor Robin) Hi, I'm doctor Robin. What brings you here?

(Patient) Hi, Dr. Robin. I feel my eyelids are sagging and dropping.

(Doctor Robin) As you age, the muscles supporting your eyelids are weaken.

(Patient) Then, what should I do to prevent eyelids from sagging?

(Doctor Robin) Double eyelid surgery can repair droopy eyelids or bags.

(Patient) I'm afraid of undergoing a procedure.

(Doctor Robin) It is done on an outpatient basis, which means it's not a complicated surgery.

(Patient) Okay. I'll go with the double eyelid surgery.

(Doctor Robin) All right. Our nurse is going to get the schedule for you.

(Patient) Thanks. Doctor.

## Dialogue 2

Nurse Patient

**Nurse:** We're going to do the operation today. You look worried, but you don't need to worry.

**Patient:** I'm trying not to. Is it going to hurt?

**Nurse:** You'll be under anesthesia. You won't feel a thing.

**Patient:** That's a relief.

**Nurse:** You'll need to sign a consent form before we can begin the procedure.

**Patient:** No problems. I'll sign it.

**Nurse:** You got a family member here?

**Patient:** Yeah, my elder sister must be around here.

## Dialogue 3

Doctor Patient

Doctor: What's the matter with your eyes?

Patient: I'm very uncomfortable because of my blurry eyesight.

Doctor: You seem to have dry eye syndrome. Do you use the computer a lot?

Patient: Yes, is that a matter?

Doctor: Of course. While staring at a computer screen for a long time, you fail to blink regularly. That can contribute to drying out your eyes.

Patient: Oh, I see. I wonder if I can have the LASIC eye surgery.

Doctor: You need to make an appointment for an examination to know if you satisfy all the requisites?

Patient: That sounds great.

Doctor: Okay. Our nurse will let you know your examination schedule.

Patient: Thank you, sir.

# Dialogue 4

Patient Doctor

Doctor: I recently had double eyelid surgery.

Patient: Why did you decide to have double eyelid surgery?

Doctor: It's because I had problems reading and my doctor recommended it.

Patient: What did your eyes look like before the surgery?

Doctor: My eyes looked very small and I didn't have a crease on my eyelids.

Patient: Why did you have second thoughts about the surgery at first?

Doctor: I didn't want my friends to think I was concerned about beauty.

Patient: I think having the surgery is a good decision you've made.

## Comprehension Check-Up

**Write the answer to the question in English.**

Q1. Hi, I'm doctor Robin. What brings you here?

A1. ______________________________________.

Q2. What should I do to prevent eyelids from sagging?

A2. ______________________________________.

Q3. Is the surgery going to hurt?

A3. ______________________________________.

Q4. You got a family member here?

A4. ______________________________________.

Q5. What's the matter with your eyes?

A5. ______________________________________.

Q6. What did your eyes look like before the surgery?

A6. ______________________________________.

Q7. Why did you have second thoughts about the surgery at first?

A7. ______________________________________.

## Translate into English

1. 무슨 일로 오셨습니까?

2. 눈의 처짐을 막으려면 어떻게 해야 하나요?

3. 나는 수술 받는 것이 두렵습니다.

4. 당신은 마취를 하게 될 것입니다.

5. 당신 눈에 무슨 문제가 있나요?

6. 우리 간호사가 당신에게 검사 일정을 알려줄 겁니다.

7. 나는 최근에 쌍꺼풀 수술을 받았습니다.

## Vocabulary Hunting

**Fill in the space for the word that fits best in the sentence.**

(decide, feel, crease, uncomfortable, nurse, prevent, contribute)

1. I didn't have a (                ) on my eyelids.

2. Why did you (                ) to have double eyelid surgery?

3. That can (                ) to drying out your eyes.

4. What should I do to (                ) eyelids from sagging?

5. I'm very (                ) because of my blurry eyesight.

6. You'll be under anesthesia. You won't (                ) a thing.

7. Our (                ) will let you know your examination schedule.

# Grammar Test 7

## 7. 분사 (Participle)

### ● Key Points

1. 분사는 준동사의 일종으로 형용사의 역할을하며 현재분사(동사원형+~ing)와 과거분사(동사원형+~ed)가 있다.
2. 현재분사는 능동과 진행의 뜻을 지니며 과거분사는 수동과 완료의 뜻을 지닌다.
3. 감정을 나타내는 동사들(please, excite, bore, annoy, surprise, astonish, satisfy, disappoint)은 사물이 주어일 때는 현재분사를 쓰고, 사람이 주어일 때는 과거분사를 쓴다.

## Choose the best form to fill the gap

**1. Who is that woman ________ glasses?**

① to wear ② wearing

③ wears ④ worn

**2. The movie was very ________, so we fell asleep.**

① boring ② bore

③ bored ④ being bored

**3. ________, Hemingway's best novel isn't The Old Man and the Sea.**

① Frankly speak ② We speaking frankly

③ Frankly to speak ④ Frankly speaking

**4. ________ by the decision, the lawyer quickly left the courtroom.**

① Having angered ② Being angry

③ Angered ④ Angering

**5. ________ a dancer herself, she has excellent posture.**

① Having being ② Being

③ Having be ④ To be

# Vocabulary Test 7

**1. What do you do in your ________ time?**

① leisure ② freely

③ excite ④ spending

**2. He was amazed by the ________ beauty of the painting.**

① available ② specialize

③ notice ④ overwhelming

**3. You should ________ with your doctor before starting a new exercise program.**

① consult ② give

③ speech ④ relax

**4. This scientific ________ is published twice a year.**

① issue ② journal

③ manuscript ④ working

**5. This medicine will ________ your pain quickly.**

① relieve ② vaccinate

③ take a break ④ cool

# Unit 8 Sightseeing

# Vocabulary

- fantastic 환상적인
- information 정보, 자료, 소식
- leaflet 전단지, 광고지(낱장으로 된 인쇄물)

cf. pamphlet 광고책자, brochure(안내, 광고용)책자, booklet 소책자(slim book)

- recommend 추천하다.
- downtown 시내 cf outskirts 도시 외곽
- admission fee 입장료 cf. fare 교통요금
- destination 목적지
- individually 개인적으로
- transportation 교통(수단)
- book 예약하다

## Dialogue 1

Miss Jeong, have you ever been to Jeju Island?

Yes, I have once.

Really? When did you go?

I went there three years ago.

How was it?

It was great! The beaches were lovely and Olle Route was fantastic to walk. If possible, I want to visit again.

Did you have Halla mountain climbing?

Of course. I climbed to the top!

Great! I'm glad you had a good time.

## Dialogue 2

Tourist information officer / Tourist

Tourist information officer: Good afternoon. How can I help you?

Tourist: Could you give me some information about the city?

Tourist information officer: No problem. How long are you going to stay here?

Tourist: I think one day is enough for a day trip in seoul.

Tourist information officer: Of course. This leaflet will give you some information where to go.

Tourist: Where would you recommend?

Tourist information officer: You can do the downtown bus tour.
Then you can visit Gyeongbokgung and The Namdaemun shopping center.

Tourist: How can I get there?

Tourist information officer: You can take a bus, subway, or taxi.

Tourist: Thank you for your help.

Tourist information officer: You're welcome.

## Dialogue 3

Guide Tourist

(Tourist) I'd like to get some information about day tour of the city.
Can I get a city map?

(Guide) Certainly, sir. Here you are.

(Tourist) May I ask you something?
I'd like to have a special night tour today. Is it possible?

(Guide) Yes, you can. The cost will be 60 dollars each person.
It includes admission fee and transportation.
And then how many people will join the special tour?

(Tourist) Most of us will join it. What time do we have to start from here?

(Guide) In front of the hotel at 7 p. m. tomorrow.

(Tourist) And when will we return to the hotel?

(Guide) At 11 p. m.

(Tourist) Okay, I'll book a tour bus for tomorrow.

## Dialogue 4

Tourist Guide

**Tourist:** Where is the destination today?

**Guide:** Today we are going to visit the palace Gyeongbokgung and National Museum. And then we will go to the shopping center.

**Tourist:** I wonder if we should go individually or together.

**Guide:** We will move together, until we arrive the shopping center.
You can have some time to buy something for an hour.
After that, we will go back to the hotel.

**Tourist:** Okay, I see.

## Comprehension Check-Up

**Answer the following sentences.**

Q1. May I speak to Mr. Kim?

A1. ____________________________________________.

Q2. When did you go?

A2. ____________________________________________.

Q3. How long are you going to stay here?

A3. ____________________________________________.

Q4. Could you give me some information?

A4. ____________________________________________.

Q5. How can I get to the shopping center?

A5. ____________________________________________.

Q6. Can I get a city map?

A6. ____________________________________________.

Q7. Where is the destination today?

A7. ____________________________________________.

## Translate into English

1. 저는 산꼭대기까지 등반 했습니다.

______________________________________________

2. 저는 3년 전에 제주도에 가봤습니다.

______________________________________________

3. 이곳에 얼마나 오래 머무르실 겁니까?

______________________________________________

4. 언제 호텔로 돌아옵니까?

______________________________________________

5. 비용은 각각 60달러입니다.

______________________________________________

6. 쇼핑 후에 스케줄이 어떻게 됩니까?

______________________________________________

7. 우리 대다수가 그 미팅에 참석할 것입니다.

______________________________________________

## Vocabulary Hunting

**Fill in the blank with the proper word.**

(destination, transportation, downtown, information, fantastic , recommend, leaflet)

1. Call (          ) and ask for her phone number.

2. I (          ) that the work (should) be done at once.

3. Where is the final (          ) of this train?

4. This (          ) will give you some information where to go.

5. It includes admission fee and (          ).

6. It was great! The beaches were lovely and Olle Route was (          ) to walk.

7. You can do the (          ) bus tour.

# Grammar Test 8

## 8. 명사 (Noun)

**Key Points**

1. 사람, 사물을 나타내는 이름으로서 문장에서 주어, 목적어, 보어의 역할을 한다.
2. 셀 수 없는 불가산 명사는 항상 단수 취급하며 단수동사로 받는다.
   furniture(가구) information(정보) baggage/luggage(수화물, 짐) evidence(증거) advice(충고) equipment(장비)
3. 집합명사 (class, family, people 등)는 집합체 전체를 하나로 생각할 때는 단수로 받고, 그 집합체를 이루는 개개의 구성원을 생각할 때는 군집명사라 하여 복수로 받는다.

## Choose the best form to fill the gap

**1. They went to the store to buy ________ stationery.**

① some ② many

③ a ④ a few

**2. The police ________ searching the apartment now.**

① is ② are

③ will be ④ shall be

**3. The company will have job ________ next month.**

① opens ② open

③ openings ④ opened

**4. He got a ________ for driving too fast on the highway.**

① change ② charge

③ prize ④ ticket

**5. I took ________ on the business trip.**

① lots of baggage ② lots of baggages

③ many baggages ④ a baggage

# Vocabulary Test 8

**1. The test will require your complete __________.**

① result ② preparation

③ target ④ transition

**2. Our service is to meet customer's __________.**

① supervisor ② purpose

③ search ④ circumstance

**3. Formal ________ is recommended for today's dinner reception.**

① food ② device

③ dress ④ shoes

**4. Our manager will deny my ________ for a new computer.**

① transition ② request

③ current ④ launch

**5. The ________ gave me good information about the matter.**

① advisor ② advising

③ advise ④ person.

# Unit 9 Restaurant

# Vocabulary

| | |
|---|---|
| order | 주문하다 |
| option | 선택 cf. choose |
| absolutely | 전적으로 |
| sticky | 끈적거리는 |
| meal | 식사 cf. dinner, lunch, breakfast |
| full | 가득 찬, 꽉 찬 (예약이) |
| reservation | 예약 make a reservation 예약하다 cf. book |
| take out | 가져가다 |
| onion | 양파 |
| sweet pepper | 피망 |
| garlic | 마늘 |
| available | 이용할 수 있는, 유효한 |
| plate | 접시 |
| adhesive | 접착의, 들러붙는 |

## Dialogue 1

May I order now?

Yes, I'm ready.

Can I get the Cheeseburger?

Would you like the burger with some tomato in the middle?

Yes, please.

And the fries with it, too?

Can I get the garlic fries?

Of course.

What are the options?

Coke, brocoli or a side salad.
For an additional charge, you can get onion rings, sweet potato fries and garlic fries.

Then can I get onion rings and sweet pepper sauce? And also coke, please.

Absolutely.

## Dialogue 2

I got the chili cheeseburger and coke. Anything else for right now?

Please bring me wet napkins because my glass is sticky.

Wait a moment please. I'll bring it right away.
Here are napkins. How's everything?

Very good.

All right. Please enjoy your meal.

Thank you very much.

May I take this plate out of the way?

Yes, you may. Thank you.

A few more fries for you?

I'm good. I'm full. Thank you.

## Dialogue 3

Hi! How many people are in your party?

Hi! We are three.

Did you make a reservation?

No, I didn't. Don't you have any seat available?

The seats are full now. It's going to be a 15-minute wait.

That's fine.

Can I have your name?

Mr. Jeong.
Can we get a high chair for my baby?

Of course.

How many people are ahead of us?

There are two.
Thank you for waiting. Follow me. please.

# Dialogue 4

Hi! Thank you for choosing Starbucks. How may I help you?

Hi! Can I get a tall size Americano please?

Yes, of course. What else for you today?

Can I get that hot in a grande cup please?

Okay. For here or to go?

I'll take it to go.

## Comprehension Check-Up

**Answer the following sentences.**

Q1. May I order now?

A1. ________________________________________.

Q2. How's everything?

A2. ________________________________________.

Q3. May I take this plate out of the way?

A3. ________________________________________.

Q4. Don't you have any seat available?

A4. ________________________________________.

Q5. How many people are ahead of us?

A5. ________________________________________.

Q6. For here or to go?

A6. ________________________________________.

## Translate into English

1. 지금 주문해도 될까요?

2. 잠시만 기다려 주세요.

3. 그릇을 가져가도 될까요?

4. 15분 정도 기다리셔야 해요.

5. 제 아이를 위해 높은 의자 좀 얻을 수 있을까요?

6. 저희 앞에 몇 명의 사람이 기다리고 있나요?

7. 드시고 가시나요? 가지고 가시나요?

## Vocabulary Hunting

**Fill in the blank with the proper word.**

(option, absolutely, napkin, sticky, meal, available)

1. All right. Please enjoy your _______ .

2. Please bring me wet ________ because my glass is sticky.

3. This service is _________ 24-hours a day.

4. I refused his offer __________ .

5. This night cream is a white, _________ substance.

6. You have the __________ of marrying her or not.

# Grammar Test 9

## 9. 한정사(Determiner)

**Key Points**

1. 명사 앞에 붙어서 명사를 한정해주는 역할을 한다.
2. 한정사는 관사(a, an, the), 인칭대명사의 소유격(my your, his, her 등), 지시형용사(this, that 등), 부정형용사(some, any, each, my, your, every 등), 수량형용사(many, much, few, little 등) 등이 있다.
3. 관사의 용법을 잘 이해하고, 수에만 쓰이는 것(many, few), 양에만 쓰이는 것(much, little)을 암기한다.

## Choose the best form to fill the gap

**1. I usually drink three cups of coffee ________ day.**

① all ② a
③ the ④ some

**2. ________ people want to stop smoking.**

① much ② many
③ every ④ little

**3. It is ________ that I'd like to go on a picnic.**

① so lovely a day ② too lovely a day
③ such a lovely a day ④ a lovely day such

**4. ________ book about the movie sells well in the bookstore.**

① The new ② One newly
③ The newly ④ New

**5. Everyone should do ________ best to solve the problem.**

① our ② their
③ its ④ his

# Vocabulary Test 9

**1. If you need more information, call the __________ desk.**

① question ② asking

③ serving ④ service

**2. I took __________ on the business trip.**

① lots of baggage ② lots of baggages

③ many baggages ④ a baggage

**3. Everyone thinks that the plane __________ to LA is expensive.**

① fee ② fare

③ rare ④ money

**4. She has __________ money to buy a large house.**

① enough ② very

③ so ④ such

**5. __________ your seat belt whenever you drive your car.**

① Fasten ② Open

③ Take ④ carefully

Breakthrough English

# Unit 10 Rent A Car

# Vocabulary

- subcompact car 경차

compact car 소형차 / midsize car 중형차 / full-size car 대형차

- driver's license 운전면허증
- deposit 예치금 예탁금 보증금 따위
- insurance 보험

Full insurance 종합보험 liability insurance 책임보험 health insurance 의료보험

- insurance Coverage 보험의 보장 범위
- reservation 예약
- pick (it) up (렌트카를) 인수하다
- drop (it) off (렌트카를) 반납하다
- rent it here and leave it there 렌트한 차를 제3의 장소에서 반납하는 방식
- unlimited miles 주행거리의 제한이 없는 렌트카 = unlimited free miles

## Dialogue 1

I'd like to rent a car.

What kind of cars do you want?

Subcompact car, please.

How long?

For a week, please.

Show me your credit card and your driver's license, please.

Sure, here you are.

## Dialogue 2

I need to rent a car.

Which model do you want?

BMW, please. What's the rental charge?

We charge 150 dollars a day and 50cents per mile.

How much is the deposit?

50$.

How about insurance?

Full insurance.

Great. I'll take it.

## Dialogue 3

Where should I return the car?

Is your rental system carried out on a 'rent it here and leave it there' basis?

Sure, that's the way we do. Would you like limited or unlimited miles?

I'd like the unlimited miles.

Would you like the optional insurance coverage?

No, thanks.

## Dialogue 4

How may I help you?

I'm here to rent a car.

Did you make a reservation?

Yes, I made a reservation for a Carnival.

How long do you want to keep it?

I'll have it for 3days. And then can I drive one way?

Yes, you can pick it up here and drop it off in another city.

Ok, let's go to walk around the car.

## Comprehension Check-Up

**Answer the following sentences.**

Q1. What kind of cars do you want?

A1. ______________________________.

Q2. What's the rental charge?

A2. ______________________________.

Q3. How much is the deposit?

A3. ______________________________.

Q4. I'm here to rent a car.

A4. ______________________________.

Q5. How long do you want to keep it?

A5. ______________________________.

Q6. Did you make a reservation?

A6. ______________________________.

## Translate into English

1. 차를 렌트하고 싶습니다.

2. 운전면허증을 보여주세요.

3. 차를 둘러보러 갑시다.

4. 보험은 어떻게 되나요?

5. 저는 속도 제한이 있는 걸로 하겠습니다.

6. 그것으로 할께요.

## Vocabulary Hunting

**Fill in the blank with the proper word.**

(deposit, insurance-coverage, reservation, pick (it) up, drop (it) off)

1. Do you have medical _________ ?

2. Can I reserve a grey one and __________ next week, please?

3. _________ one dollar and push the button.

4. Yes, you can pick it up here and __________ in another city.

5. When your __________ is confirmed, we'll call you.

# Grammar Test 10

## 10. 형용사(Adjective)

**● Key Points**

1. 형용사는 명사를 수식하며 보충 설명하는 역할을 한다.
2. 명사 앞에서 한정적 용법으로만 쓰이는 형용사는 live, only, main, elder, former, drunken 등이 있고, 서술적 용법으로 동사 뒤에서 보어로 쓰이는 형용사는 alive, asleep, afraid, awake, aware, alike 등이 있다.
3. 수량형용사

   many a + 단수명사 + 단수동사 (많은)

   many + 복수명사 + 복수동사 (많은)

   a number of + 복수명사 + 복수동사 (많은)

   the number of + 복수명사 + 단수동사 (~의 수)

## Choose the best form to fill the gap

**1. The Korean dream does not come to those who fall ________.**

① sleep ② asleep

③ sleeping ④ slept

**2. The guerrillas' intention is to capture him ________.**

① alive ② to live

③ to be alive ④ living

**3. Because the family is poor, the children have ________ clothes.**

① a little ② little

③ a few ④ few

**4. " Did you enjoy the movie?" "No, It was ________."**

① very bored ② much boring

③ much bored ④ very boring

**5. Some ________ CEOs usually have their own ideas.**

① success ② successful

③ successive ④ succeed

# Vocabulary Test 10

**1. The new manager has __________ come at the meeting .**

① yet ② still
③ already ④ no

**2. He was __________ invited to the party.**

① very ② kindly
③ kind ④ kindness

**3. We ____________ the directions carefully, so that we did not make a mistake.**

① said ② followed
③ see ④ hold

**4. I would like to see you in the __________ future.**

① near ② well
③ succeed ④ complete

**5. The parking spaces are __________ for guest of the restaurant.**

① reserved ② the good
③ clear ④ reservation

# Unit 11 Hairshop

# Vocabulary

| | |
|---|---|
| • perm | 파마 cf. permanent 영구적인 |
| • appointment | 약속 |
| • loose | 헐거운 느슨한 |
| • curl | 곱슬머리 |
| • convenient | 편리한 |
| • conditioner | (헤어)유연제 |
| • damage | 손상 |
| • rod | 막대기 perm rod 파마봉 |
| • solution | 액체, 해결책 perm solution 파마약 |
| • porous | 다공성의 |
| • treatment | 치료, 처치 |
| • dye | 염색하다 |
| • complement | 보충하다 |
| • chemical | 화학적인 |
| • prepare | 준비하다 |

## Dialogue 1

Hair Dresser / Customer

Hair Dresser: Hi, It's been a long time.

Customer: How have you been?

Hair Dresser: Very well. Did you have an appointment for a perm today?

Customer: Of course, I did.

Hair Dresser: What type of perm would you like to try ?

Customer: I'd like to change my hair style.

Hair Dresser: Oh, I see. Would you like to see pictures of the popular style?

Customer: Yes, please.
Let me see.... I've always had straight hair. But the loose curls on this page might work for me.

Hair Dresser: I think that it is a perfect choice.
This style looks very natural and modern these days.

Customer: OK, I'll take it.

## Dialogue 2

Hair Dresser　Customer

(Customer) Hello! I need a perm today. What time shall I make an appointment for?

(Hair Dresser) 2 p. m. will be convenient.

(Customer) I need a new hair style.

(Hair Dresser) How would you like your hair cut?

(Customer) Just do whatever is best for me. And please cut a little more off the sides.

(Hair Dresser) Please change into this gown and get into the chair.
O. K. Your hair is really dry. You need a good conditioner.
Have you shampooed today?

(Hair Dresser) Yes. I used the shampoo and rinse specially designed for damaged hair.

(Hair Dresser) I see.
Now I'll wind the perm rods and then apply the perm solution. .....
It's done. Let me wash your hair.
The wave looks good.

(Customer) Thank you for your service today.

(Hair Dresser) It's my pleasure.

## Dialogue 3

Hair Dresser　Customer

How should I style it?

Can you give me a loose and natural wave?

Yes. But your hair seems to be porous and the perm style does not last long. Is it okay?

That's fine.

When was the last time you had a perm?

Three months ago.

Let me give you a perm after the treatment.
Did you rinse your hair today?

Yes, I shampooed it.

O. K. I'll start your treatment now.
Please tell me if you need anything.

O. K. Thanks.

## Dialogue 4

Hair Dresser　Customer

Hair Dresser: You look good today.

Customer: Thank you. Can you dye my hair?

Hair Dresser: Your hair was dyed dark brown before.
What color do you want?

Customer: What color would be good for me?

Hair Dresser: A bright brown color will complement your skin tone and it will make you look younger.

Customer: That sounds good.

Hair Dresser: When was the last time you had any chemical service?

Customer: I got my hair dyed two months ago.

Hair Dresser: I got it, it will be fine to dye your hair today. Just a moment please.
I'll prepare for coloring.

Customer: O. K. Thank you.

## Comprehension Check-Up

**Answer the following sentences.**

Q1. How have you been?

A1. ______________________________________________.

Q2. What type of perm would you like to try ?

A2. ______________________________________________.

Q3. How would you like your hair cut?

A3. ______________________________________________.

Q4. Can you give me a loose and natural wave?

A4. ______________________________________________.

Q5. Please tell me if you need anything.

A5. ______________________________________________.

Q6. Can you dye my hair?

A6. ______________________________________________.

Q7. What color would be good for me?

A7. ______________________________________________.

## Translate into English

1. 저는 헤어스타일을 바꾸고 싶습니다.

2. 유행하는 스타일사진을 보시겠어요?

3. 가운으로 갈아입으시고 의자에 앉으세요.

4. 머리를 감겨드리겠습니다.

5. 마지막으로 펌하신지 얼마나 됐나요?

6. 그 머리스타일은 당신을 더 젊어보이게 할 것입니다.

7. 오늘 샴푸 하셨나요?

## Vocabulary Hunting

**Fill in the blank with the proper word.**

(trim, appointment, convenient, dye, damage, rod, solution, treatment, complement, chemical, prepare )

1. We must clean up the dioxin found in _________ waste dumps.

2. Excessive drinking does ________ to health.

3. He must be sent to hospital for __________.

4. I'd like to _______ my hair.

5. Soap water is an alkaline ___________.

6. I need to change my ___________ with Mr. Walker.

7. A good wine is a __________ to a good meal.

8. Credit cards are more _________ than cash.

9. All Students should _______ the final exam.

10. Can you put your hair into _______ ?

11. He received a fishing ______ for his birthday.

# Grammar Test 11

## 11. 부사(Adverb)

● **Key Points**

1. 부사는 동사, 형용사, 부사, 부사구 또는 문장 전체를 수식한다.
2. 빈도부사는 be동사, 조동사 뒤, 일반동사 앞에 위치한다.
3. very : 형용사 및 부사의 원급, 현재분사, 형용사화된 과거분사(tired, pleased, excited, surprised, interested, amused) 등을 수식한다.

   much : 비교급, 최상급, 과거분사, 동사, 서술적형용사(alike, alive, afraid), too, the same 등을 수식한다..

## Choose the best form to fill the gap

**1. Smoking ________ your health.**

① can affect dangerously ② can seriously affect

③ seriously can affect ④ hardly can endanger

**2. Fasten your seat belt ________ whenever you drive your car.**

① securely ② secure

③ security ④ securable

**3. Golf is becoming an ________ popular sport.**

① increasing ② increased

③ increase ④ increasingly

**4. He was ________ invited to the party.**

① kindness ② kind

③ kindly ④ kindness

**5. We must leave the party at exactly 9:00, _______ we'll be late for work.**

① for else ② other

③ else ④ otherwise

# Vocabulary Test 11

**1. Korea should ____________ its economic assistance to the country.**

① went ② increase

③ helped ④ receiving

**2. I want to buy ________ at the store.**

① some color ② a few

③ something ④ anything

**3. Most college students have ______ own cellular phone.**

① their ② his

③ her ④ its

**4. His ability is __________ in all his reports.**

① evident ② ideal

③ made ④ reveal

**5. Work hard , and you can _________ from salesperson to sales manager.**

① transfer ② advance

③ start ④ succeeded

# Unit 12 Hotel

# Vocabulary

- expect　기대하다
- arrive　도착하다 arrival 도착 / departure 출발
- rate　요금(rental rate)

  charge 이용요금 (service charge / water charge 수도요금)

  fee 요금(an entrance fee 입장료 / tuition fee 등록금)

  fare 운임(taxi fare / return fare 왕복운임)
- tax　세금
- registration　등록
- pressed　다림질된
- extra charge　부가서비스 요금
- overcharge　추가요금
- add　추가하다

## Dialogue 1

Reservation clerk / Guest

**Reservation clerk:** Hotel Shilla Reservation. How may I help you?

**Guest:** I'd like to reserve a room for two nights.

**Reservation clerk:** When do you expect to arrive here?

**Guest:** I'll be there at 8:00 p.m.

**Reservation clerk:** Hold the line, please. I'll check on that. What kind of room would you like, ma'am?

**Guest:** A single room please. What's the room rate?

**Reservation clerk:** A single room is $100, a night including tax and service charge.

**Guest:** Okay. I'll take it.

## Dialogue 2

Reservation clerk / Guest

**Reservation clerk:** Good afternoon, ma'am. How may I help you?

**Guest:** I have reservation here.

**Reservation clerk:** May I have your name or reservation number?

**Guest:** Miss Jeong.

**Reservation clerk:** Wait a minute, please. Your room is 1004. It is a single room. Could you fill out this registration card? And you should deposit $500.

**Guest:** Sure, here you are.

**Reservation clerk:** I hope you enjoy your stay here.

## Dialogue 3

Reservation clerk　Guest

Reservation clerk: This is Housekeeping, may I help you?

Guest: Yes. Could you send someone to my room?

Reservation clerk: May I ask what the problem is?

Guest: I'd like to have some shirts cleaned and pressed.

Reservation clerk: Okay. I'll send you someone as soon as possible.

<Room>

Reservation clerk: Laundry service, may I come in?

Guest: Sure. I need to have these shirts cleaned and pressed.

Reservation clerk: Okay, ma'am. Could you fill out the laundry form, please?

Guest: Sure, here you are. When can I get it back?

Reservation clerk: It usually takes a few days.

Guest: I see. How much does it cost per piece?

Reservation clerk: It depends. It's usually 20 dollars a piece.

Guest: Can I get it back tomorrow morning?

Reservation clerk: Yes, but you have to pay an extra charge.

Guest: No problem.

## Dialogue 4

Reservation clerk / Guest

**Reservation clerk:** Good afternoon, sir. May I help you?

**Guest:** I'd like to check out. My room number is 1004. How much do I pay you?

**Reservation clerk:** Wait a moment, sir. Let me check your bill. It comes to $200 altogether. Cash or a credit card?

**Guest:** Cash, please. Here you go. But I think it is more than I expected.

**Reservation clerk:** Do you know that an overcharge will be added to your bill when you check out late?

**Guest:** I didn't know that. What percent will be added?

**Reservation clerk:** It is added about thirty percent in an hour.

**Guest:** I see.

## Comprehension Check-Up

**Answer the following sentences.**

Q1. When do you expect to arrive here?

A1. ______________________________________________.

Q2. What kind of room would you like, sir?

A1. ______________________________________________.

Q3. What's the room rate?

A3. ______________________________________________.

Q4. Could you fill out this registration card?

A4. ______________________________________________.

Q5. Could you send someone to my room?

A5. ______________________________________________.

Q6. Could you fill out the laundry form, please?

A6. ______________________________________________.

Q7. Can I get it back tomorrow morning?

A7. ______________________________________________.

## Translate into English

1. 저는 2일 동안 머물 방 하나를 예약하고 싶습니다.

2. 당신은 추가요금을 지불하셔야합니다.

3. 제 예상보다 비용이 더 많이 나왔네요.

4. 제 셔츠를 세탁 맡기고 싶습니다.

5. 가능한 빨리 사람을 보내겠습니다.

6. 문제가 무엇인지 여쭈어 봐도 될까요?

7. 숙박계를 써주시겠습니까?

## Vocabulary Hunting

**Fill in the blank with the proper word.**

(expect, rate, tax, registration, overcharge)

1. Will you fill out this __________ form?

2. I bought cosmetics at a ________ free shop.

3. What time do you _______ him home?

4. The taxi driver tried to ___________ me.

5. A single room, please. What's the room _______ ?

   The ______ is 50 dollars a day.

# Grammar Test 12

## 12. 전치사(preposition)

**● Key Points**

1. 전치사는 명사나 명사 상당어구와 결합하여 형용사구 혹은 부사구를 이룬다.
   The books on the desk are mine. (형용사구)
   Put the book on the desk, please. (부사구)
2. for : 숫자로 시작되는 기간 앞에 쓰임
   during : 구체적인 명사 앞에 쓰임
   since : 현재완료시제 문장에 주로 쓰임
3. 전치사의 목적어가 동사가 될 때는 동명사이어야 한다.
   Before going to bed, you must brush your teeth.
   Thank you very much for inviting me.

## Choose the best form to fill the gap

**1. ________ his faults, he is a great poet.**

① Though ② Despite
③ For ④ With

**2. ________ a slight improvement in sales, the company is still making a loss.**

① Despite of ② In regard to
③ For ④ In spite of

**3. ________ his brother, he was indifferent to such matters.**

① Alike ② Unless
③ Despite ④ Unlike

**4. What language do you learn at school ________ French?**

① beside ② next to
③ besides ④ within

**5. She was happy ________ her lifetime.**

① during ② for
③ while ④ to

# Vocabulary Test 12

**1. I had to ________ from the company because of my health problem.**

① go ② praise
③ resign ④ fire

**2. How can I ________ the students to improve their abilities?**

① offer ② use
③ survey ④ motivate

**3. The phone is simpler to use and more ________ than that one.**

① affordable ② confidence
③ price ④ rather

**4. You can win a ________ dinner for two at the Department grand opening.**

① satisfaction ② helpful
③ moderately ④ complimentary

**5. Our country is still struggling to recover from the recent________.**

① strike ② recession
③ trend ④ finance

# Unit 13 Airport

# Vocabulary

- flights 비행편

departure 출발(take off 이륙) arrival 도착(landing 착륙) local time 도착지 시간

- boarding pass 탑승권

check-in 탑승수속 baggage check-in counter 짐 발송 수속 대 immigration 출입국 심사

boarding 탑승 passenger 탑승객 crew 승무원(captain 기장 / steward stewardess

- round trip ticket(= return ticket) 왕복 승차권

one way ticket(= single ticket) 편도 승차권

- certainly = sure 물론입니다
- overhead 머리 위쪽
- bin 빈 통
- aisle 좁은 통로
- belongings 짐 소지품 baggage claim (공항에서) 짐 찾는 곳
- tray 쟁반 in-flight meals 기내식(= in-flight food and beverage)
- seatbelt 안전벨트
- upright 곧게 세운, 곧추선
- cooperation 협조

## Dialogue 1

Passenger Reservation Clerk

Hello, Is this Korean Air Reservations?

Yes, sir. How can I help you?

I'd like to reserve the flights to L.A. on May 10th.

How many people will be traveling?

Just myself.

Ok. Economy or business class, sir?

Economy, please.

Your reservation is made for Korean Air 707 on May 10th.

All right. Thank you.

You're welcome. Thank you for calling Korean Air.

## Dialogue 2

Passenger Reservation

Good morning. May I help you, sir?

I want to get a ticket for Los Angles.

Did you make a reservation?

No I didn't.

When would you like to fly?

On May 10th.

We have just two open seats. One at 9 a.m. and the other at 5 p.m.

I'd rather take the 5 p.m. flight.

Would you like a round trip ticket?

Yes, please.

Thank you for flying Korean Air.

## Dialogue 3

Stewardess Passenger

**Stewardess:** Good morning. May I have your boarding pass, please?

**Passenger:** Sure, here you are.

**Stewardess:** Thank you. Your seat number is 10C. Please take the aisle to the right. May I help you with your belongings?

**Passenger:** Yes, please.

**Stewardess:** Could you put your bags in the overhead bin or under the seat in front of you?

**Passenger:** No problem. And can I have a glass of water?

**Stewardess:** Certainly, sir. I'll get it for you right away. Here is your drink, sir.

**Passenger:** Thank you.

# Dialogue 4

Stewardess Passenger

**Stewardess:** Excuse me, ma'am. We'll be serving dinner soon. Would you mind opening your tray table, please?

**Passenger:** What's the meal today?

**Stewardess:** We have Korean style Bibimbab and meat with rice.

**Passenger:** Bibimbab, please.

**Stewardess:** What would you like to drink? We have coffee, orange juice.

**Passenger:** Coffee and water, please.

**Stewardess:** Here you are. Enjoy your meal, ma'am.

(3 hours later)

**Stewardess:** We'll be landing soon. Please fasten your seatbelt and return your seat back and tray table to the upright position.

**Passenger:** Okay.

**Stewardess:** Thank you for your cooperation.

## Comprehension Check-Up

**Answer the following sentences.**

Q1. Is this Korean Air Reservations?

A1. ______________________________.

Q2. How many people will be traveling?

A1. ______________________________.

Q3. Did you make a reservation?

A3. ______________________________.

Q4. When would you like to fly?

A4. ______________________________.

Q5. Would you like a round trip ticket?

A5. ______________________________.

Q6. May I help you with your belongings?

A6. ______________________________.

Q7. What's the meal today?

A7. ______________________________.

## Translate into English

1. 물 한잔 주시겠어요?

2. 탑승권을 보여주시겠어요?

3. 어떤 음료로 드릴까요?

4. 안전벨트를 매주세요.

5. 좌석을 원위치해주시고 트레이 테이블을 똑바로 해주시길 바랍니다.

6. 곧 착륙하겠습니다.

7. 오른쪽 통로로 가세요.

## Vocabulary Hunting

**Fill in the blank with the proper word.**

(flights, boarding-pass, aisle, belongings, tray, upright, cooperation)

1. The ugly face man stretched his leg out in the ________ of the airplane.

2. The stewardess is serving lunch on a _______ .

3. An _________ body is the sign of confidence.

4. And don't forget any of your _________ .

5. Everyone, thank you for your _____________ .

6. All _______ are on service without any delay.

7. Excuse me, but would you please show me your ______________ ?

# Grammar Test 13

## 13. 관계사(Relative)

**● Key Points**

1. 관계대명사는 바로 앞의 명사(선행사)에 대해 보충 설명을 하는 형용사절이다.
2. 관계대명사 that : 선행사가 '사람+사물', 최상급, all, every, something, everything일 때, 명사 앞에 한정사로 서수(the first), the only, the same 등이 올 때 that을 쓴다.
3. 복합 관계대명사는 '관계대명사+ever'의 형태로 양보(~일지라도, ~든지)의 뜻을 지니며 선행사를 포함하는 관계대명사이다.

## Choose the best form to fill the gap

**1. He is seeking ________ he thinks is real and beautiful.**

① what ② which
③ that ④ where

**2. The care ________ he did his work surprised me.**

① of which ② with that
③ with which ④ such as

**3. This morning, I met a woman ________ father died last Friday.**

① whose ② who
③ whom ④ who's

**4. She was the only person ________ came into the room.**

① what ② that
③ which ④ whom

**5. ________ comes first is supposed to get the prize.**

① Who ② Anyone
③ Those who ④ Whoever

# Vocabulary Test 13

**1. This firm needs to ________ its system for the project.**

① place ② decide

③ reflect ④ streamline(간소화하다)

**2. Senior managers have the ________ to hire and fire employees.**

① stance ② statement

③ emphasis ④ authority

**3. We are waiting for a(an) _______ of the company's financial situation.**

① assessment ② reputation

③ understanding ④ cooperation

**4. Many business owners are worrying about ________ changes in tax policy.**

① potential ② independent

③ good ④ confront

**5. Be careful when you _________ power tools.**

① observe ② storage

③ operate ④ run

# Unit 14 Job Interview and Business English

# Vocabulary

- personnel manager (기업체에서) 인사담당자
- applicant 지원자 / apply 지원하다, 신청하다
- briefly 간략히
- introduce 소개하다
- position 직책
- prospects 전망 / 장래성
- qualifications 자격
- certificate 자격증, 증명서, 면허증
- personality 성격
- outgoing and sociable 외향적이고 사회적인
- customer 고객

  consumer 소비자 regular 단골손님 purchaser 구매자 buyer 구매자
- complaint 불만
- conflicts 충돌, 갈등
- celebrate 축하하다
- anniversary 기념일(매년 있는) / 25th anniversary 25주년 기념일
- hold 개최하다 / We are holding ~ 우리가 ~을 개최할 예정이다
- express 표현하다

- appreciation　감탄 / express one's appreciation 감사를 표하다

  appreciate 진가를 알아보다, 고맙게 생각하다

| | |
|---|---|
| • extend | 넓히다 |
| • look forward to | 고대하다 |
| • delight | 기쁨 |
| • your kind invitation | 당신의 호의적인 초대 |
| • recognition | 알아봄, 인정, 인식 |
| • dedicated | 헌신적인 |
| • outstanding | 탁월한 |
| • commitment | 활동, 실행 |
| • volunteer | 자발적인 지원자 |
| • instructor | 코치, 강사 |

## Dialogue 1

Personnel manager · Applicant

**Personnel manager:** Would you tell me your name?

**Applicant:** Jisoo Leem.

**Personnel manager:** Miss Leem, please introduce yourself briefly.

**Applicant:** Yes, sir. I was born in Pyeongtaek on October 1st, 1991. I graduated from Kookje university and majored in Hotel and Tourism Service.

**Personnel manager:** Have you ever had any job experience?

**Applicant:** I worked at Kookje hotel for 2 years and had an internship in Singapore for 6 months.

**Personnel manager:** And what was your position there?

**Applicant:** I worked at the Front Desk.

**Personnel manager:** Thank you. We will call you when we decide.

## Dialogue 2

Personnel manager　Applicant

**Personnel manager:** What made you decide to apply for our company?

**Applicant:** Well, I wanted to get a job where I can use my major. Especially, I think that the prospects for this field are very bright.

**Personnel manager:** Do you have any licences or qualifications?

**Applicant:** Yes, I have a certificate of tour conductor.

**Personnel manager:** What do you think of your personality?

**Applicant:** I am very outgoing and sociable. So, I am deeply interested in working in the customer service area.

**Personnel manager:** How would you handle customer complaints?

**Applicant:** I think communication is the key point to ease up most conflicts and I try to put myself in the customers' shoes.

**Personnel manager:** Thank you for your good answers. The interview is over.

**Applicant:** Thank you very much.

# Business Letter

## Case 1. The 25th Anniversary of Jin Company Invitation

Dear Dr. Jeong

To celebrate the 25th anniversary of Jin Company, we are holding a dinner party at the W Hotel in Seoul from 8 to 10 p.m. on Friday, December 20, 2017.

You are invited to the party so that we can express our sincere appreciation for the support. You have extended to us for many years.

We do hope that you will be able to join us and look forward to seeing you at the party.

Sincerely yours.

Jin Company

Jin Leem

President

## Case 2. Acception of Invitation

I am delighted to accept your kind invitation to dinner party with you on Friday, the fifth of May, at 8p.m. and I am looking forward to that day with the great pleasure.

## Case 3. Refusal of Invitation

We are very sorry to say that we are unable to accept your kind invitation on Wednesday, sixth of June, as we have another meeting for that day.

## Case 4. Certificate of Appreciation

**Anthony K. Wade**

In recognition of your dedicated service and outstanding commitment as a volunteer English instructor in Kookje University, we gladly present this certificate.

May 25, 2017

International Relations Center

Kookje University

## Comprehension Check-Up

**Answer the following sentences.**

Q1. Please introduce yourself briefly.

A1. ________________________________________________.

Q2. Have you ever had any job experience?

A2. ________________________________________________.

Q3. What was your position there?

A3. ________________________________________________.

Q4. What made you decide to apply for our company?

A4. ________________________________________________.

Q5. Do you have any licences or qualifications?

A5. ________________________________________________.

Q6. What do you think of your personality?

A6. ________________________________________________.

## Translate into English

1. 결정이 되면 알려드리겠습니다.

2. 제 전공을 살릴 수 있는 직업을 얻기를 원합니다.

3. 우리는 당신이 우리와 함께하기를 바랍니다.

4. 저는 외향적이고 사교적입니다.

5. 당신은 고객의 불만을 어떻게 처리하십니까?

6. 우리는 그날 다른 미팅이 있어요.

7. 저는 기쁜 마음으로 그날을 고대하겠습니다.

## Vocabulary Hunting

**Fill in the blank with the proper word.**

(applicant, briefly, introduce, certificate, outgoing and sociable, complaint, celebrate, anniversary, looking forward to, volunteer, recognition, outstanding)

1. She has worked as a _________ in a day-care center.
2. He has a high school _________.
3. An __________ must pass an examination on the subject.
4. The manager received special bonus for his __________ work.
5. Angry customer has a _______ about a bad product.
6. I am _________________ that day with the great pleasure.
7. Generally, personal managers prefer ______________ people.
8. This year marks the 100th ___________ for the Kookje university.
9. I'll explain __________ about this new product.
10. He was promoted in ____________ of his achievement.
11. Let me __________ our captain. He is Mr. Robert, iron man!
12. I sent invitation card to my friend to _________ my birthday.

# Grammar Test 14

## 14. 접속사(Connection)

**● Key Points**

1. 접속사는 단어, 구, 절 문장을 서로 연결할 때 사용하는 연결어로, 등위접속사 and, but, or, for와 등위상관접속사 both A and B, either A or B, B as well as A와 종속접속사 that, if/whether(~인지 아닌지) 가 있다.
2. 부사절(양보, 시간, 이유, 원인, 조건, 목적, 결과 등)의 용법을 이해한다.
3. 접속사와 전치사의 차이를 이해한다.
   It is getting dark, for it is going to rain. (접속사)
   I stayed in America for seven days. (전치사)

## Choose the best form to fill the gap

**1. He is both kind ________ honest.**

① or ② nor

③ and ④ for

**2. ________ he had a lot of money, he was not satisfied.**

① Since ② Although

③ Despite ④ as

**3. Children cannot enter the theater ________ accompanied by their parents.**

① unless ② if

③ while ④ although

**4. I don't know ________ Susan will come back tomorrow.**

① whenever ② whereas

③ whether ④ while

**5. Drivers are dangerous if they use cell phones ________ driving.**

① unless ② as

③ while ④ by

## Vocabulary Test 14

**1. The company decided not to ________ production of this model.**

① discontinue ② continue

③ repair ④ depend

**2. There were some ___________ found in the materials received from the supplier.**

① technician ② variety

③ flaws ④ production

**3. We _______ to inform you that the flight to New York has been canceled.**

① regret ② serve

③ refer ④ sorry

**4. Access to the building will be ________.**

① escort ② fulfill

③ direct ④ restricted

**5. We hope to ________ you again in the future.**

① serve ② delay

③ enter ④ keep

## 저자소개

**정은주**(Eun Joo Jeong)
영문학 박사(세종대학교대학원 영어영문학과, 영미문학 전공)
현) 국제대학교 호텔관광과 부교수

**고인숙**(Inn Sook Koh)
영문학 박사(성균관대학교대학원 영어영문학과, 영미문학 전공)
현) 국제대학교 컴퓨터정보통신계열 부교수

## Breakthrough English

**초판 1쇄 인쇄** 2017년 8월 16일
**초판 1쇄 발행** 2017년 8월 21일

| | |
|---|---|
| **저 자** | 정은주 · 고인숙 |
| **펴낸이** | 임 순 재 |
| **펴낸곳** | **(주)한올출판사** |
| **등 록** | 제11-403호 |
| **주 소** | 서울시 마포구 모래내로 83(성산동 한올빌딩 3층) |
| **전 화** | (02) 376-4298(대표) |
| **팩 스** | (02) 302-8073 |
| **홈페이지** | www.hanol.co.kr |
| **e-메 일** | hanol@hanol.co.kr |
| **ISBN** | **979-11-5685-597-2** |